BUSINESS SUCCESS – THE ESSENTIALS

CONTENTS

Chapter 1	Where do we start?
Chapter 2	Anticipate & identify
Chapter 3	Understanding the risks
Chapter 4	Satisfying the Customer
Chapter 5	Face to face Selling
Chapter 6	Open Questions
Chapter 7	Customer requirements
Chapter 8	Profitably
Chapter 9	Getting there and staying there
Chapter 10	The S.W.O.T. analysis
Chapter 11	Secrets of Successful Advertising
Chapter 12	Getting the most out of your mailshots
Chapter 13	Cut Price Postage
Chapter 14	Selling at Exhibitions
Chapter 15	Producing a Website that really works for you
Chapter 16	Offline Advertising
Chapter 17	Search Engine Optimisation
Chapter 18	How to produce your own video
Chapter 19	How to understand and produce a Blog
Chapter 20	The Internet Selling Game
Chapter 21	Using Ebay as an opportunity to sell
Chapter 22	Avoiding feast and famine times
Chapter 23	Running your own profitable Seminars
Chapter 24	Understanding E-Books
Chapter 25	Accounts made Easy

PREFACE

Hello and welcome,

I have been running my Business "Surgery" for over 30 years now and along the way I have been able to help many hundreds of businesses start up and succeed. As a Trouble-shooter, I have also been called in to sort out a variety of problems that often related to existing businesses losing money. I really did need to do a bit of surgery to get some of them back on track.

My clear objective is to give you some important guidelines that I recommend you refer to on a regular basis that will help you to progress and prosper and save me the time and effort of having to carry out some "surgical operations" that could be quite painful.

Why bother with me?

One thing I would like to make clear. It is not unreasonable for company Directors or Proprietors of businesses to hold little faith in Business Consultants who have either never been in business themselves, or, perhaps, who did have a business a trillion years ago and are really not in keeping with modern trends and up to date business environments.

Allow me to enlighten you by saying that I also currently run an online health products distribution business and a publishing company that has been growing steadily, alongside an Ebay shop. I started with Ebay in 2004 and I have made just over 1200 transactions with a 100% written positive feedbacks from every client. Suffice to say, I am well involved with our own business as well as wearing a Business Consultancy hat.

Now that I have got that off my chest, let's press on with some tips that I would like to share with you, some of which I gained by making mistakes.
They say you learn by your mistakes. Believe me- I have learnt a lot!

Chapter 1

Where do we start?

Too many times I have come across successful Sales People who have embarked upon setting up their own business and eagerly jump in the deep end relying solely upon their sales experience, only to find that they fall down at the first hurdle because their over enthusiasm prevented them from thinking things through properly before seeing a prospect client.

A good marketing strategy is of paramount importance yet so many people think that Marketing is a posh word for Sales. **Not so!**

Before we go into what Marketing is really all about let me present to you some facts about how businesses fair in this day and age with and without a strategic approach to their business.

Strong Marketing strategy
Strong Tactical activity   =   **Business will prosper**

Strong Marketing strategy
Weak Tactical activity   =   **Business may just survive**

Weak Marketing strategy
Strong Tactical activity   =   **Business will die slowly**

Weak Marketing strategy
Weak Tactical activity   =   **Call me!**

I cannot emphasis enough the importance of understanding what marketing is about and how that knowledge, once put into practice,
Will help to put your business on the road to success.

There are five rules of Marketing that are in the definition. Please try and memorise the five elements of the definition. By having carried out all the necessary research that relates to the 5 elements, you will be on your way to success. If you miss out **any one** of those elements, you can expect a difficult time ahead.

The Definition of Marketing

is the Management process

of

ANTICIPATING, IDENTIFYING SATISFYING, CUSTOMER REQUIREMENTS, PROFITABLY

If you already have a product or service, that's great. If not, consider converting your hobby into a business or start looking at the various interests that you have that could become very useful business opportunities.

Do not be sentimentally attached to your product or service if you have found that nobody is really interested in it. Find out why and learn from the feedbacks. Conversely you may not like the product yourself but it may be a good seller!

I recall when I was working for a wholesale jewellery company, selling gold bracelets to Retail Jewellers, I came across a Pawnbroker who was quite prepared to look at the range I had to offer.
I eagerly opened up my sample case and made it clear to the retailer that he could have instant delivery. Whatever he picked, he could have immediately.

He looked at the range intently and began to remove over half of the bracelets that I had in my sample case and laid them down on the Counter. I swiftly went to my order book and readily confirmed that what was on the Counter was what he wanted.

"No" he said. "I don't want any of those". "But you seemed to like them when you laid them on the Counter" I remarked.

"Yes", he replied. "I do like them very much. But you need to know
that I have been running this business in this town for over 20 years and I have learnt that everything that I like just doesn't sell and, in most cases, what I don't like does. So please let me have what you have left in the sample case."

This guy knew his business, so who was I to argue with him. Have an open mind about products and services and spend time researching what your prospect customers like rather than relying on your own opinion.

Either way, before you embark upon spending all your advertising money, take the first important two steps of important Marketing strategies.

Chapter 2 – Anticipate & Identify

Anticipating – forecast, predict, prophesy, foretell, pre-empt.
Identifying - recognising, pinpointing, distinguishing, verifying.

To help you understand the practical requirements of "Anticipating" and "Identifying" I am going to take you through the process that I had to go through when I decided to invent my own little product called "Nek-Pak".

Years ago, when credit cards were owned by a select few. I thought about the frustration that such people would have when going abroad on holiday.

A credit card was quite precious and people would not want to leave them in the hotel safe. If they went swimming they could not exactly take the cards with them. Pick-pockets were rife and there was an element of vulnerability. So here was a problem.

Solve a problem and you could have a viable product or a service!

I invented a waterproof plastic container that contained up to 6 credit cards. It had a lid that was joined to its base by a neck-string. I **anticipated** that it could be an excellent little promotional item that could have a company logo emblazoned upon it.

Those that wore it could happily go swimming, go shopping and

6

not worry about pick-pockets as it was around their neck.

It had to say what it was. Hence **Nek-Pak.**

All sounds great so far. Get ready for a whole can of worms!

At that early stage I felt that I had ticked 2 of the 5 elements …. **anticipated** and **identified.**

But a number of other things came into play here.

Rec. Retail, Colours, Price of string. Who could make it? Cost?
What about **Trademark, Patents etc. Where** would I sell them? **How** could I sell them?

How do you base a rec. retail price on something that has never existed before? It was a tough call.

After months of further research I was able to find a plastic extruder who was prepared to sign a confidentiality agreement and come up with the kind of design that I had in mind.
The initial setting-up costs were into four figures but he agreed to amortise the costs over the spread of an order for 10,000 products.

It worked out at a net cost to me of 22p per pack plus approx. 3p per string.

We finally had the product.

We had to order a minimum of 100 units at a time per colour.

Initial trademark and patent costs through an agent proved expensive so I went to London to the patent office and saved a load of money doing it myself.

So you might think at 22p I could sell at say 99p and be happy with the profit?

Hang on. How much is it worth to the customer to have the peace of mind knowing that their credit cards will not be stolen? Much more than 99p.

I approached the Daily Telegraph and Guardian. National Newspapers that I believed would attract the type of prospect customers I was looking for.

I had a "NEK-PAK" logo in silver designed to go on every pack and arranged for 6 different colours to be made.

I did an offer in the Daily Telegraph with a little drawing of the product with a brief description and sold them at £3-50 each or two for £5.

Every order was for 2 at a time.

If you have a good product – aim high. You can always reduce later.

I subsequently negotiated a deal with Natwest Bank for a Black "Nek-Pak" with their silver logo that they gave away to their clients going abroad who took advantage of their travel insurance services. It was very successful.

I managed to tick all 5 elements.
I later moved on to consultancy work and sold the product to a company in the U.S. It was a good marketing exercise for me personally that involved elements of risk on the way. let's now look at the various levels of risk involved in operating **your** business when you sell a product.

Chapter 3 Understanding the Risks

From here on in, when I refer to a "Product" I am including a "Service".

ANSOFF'S THEORY

Existing Product entering an Existing Market Place
LOW RISK

Here you can research the existing market place, look at what other competitive products are around. Check the prices, packaging etc. and try to see if you can offer an improved product or, provided you can make a decent profit, offer a product of the same quality at a lower price. You may be able to make the product more attractive. You may be able to offer a better service. Either way, your risk is low because you already have in front of you all the necessary ingredients that have already covered **Anticipate** & **Identify.**

New Product entering an Existing Market Place
HIGHER RISK

If you already have a list of happy customers, you can offer them a new product that they will, at least, have a look at because they already have a track record with you and you have built up a relationship already.
It may be a product or service that has shown success elsewhere. This level of risk is although higher, is reasonably comfortable if you have carried out your first two elements correctly.

Existing Product entering a New Market Place
HIGHER RISK

Consider offering your product or service abroad for the first time. Here you need to consider a number of new factors.

Price; Colour; Local Customs; Religious Dos & Don'ts; Rates of Exchange; Shipping costs; Language etc.

Here you have a situation where no matter how much research you have done for your existing market, you really have to go back to square one to really be sure that you can correctly tick **Anticipate** and **Identify**

New Product entering a New Market Place
HIGHEST RISK
This is the "NEK-PAK" scenario. A new invention.
Lots of things to consider before you spend all your money.

Chapter 4 – Satisfying the Customer

Satisfying – pleasing, comforting, gratifying, fulfilling.

We are now embarking on the area of sales and how we can satisfy our Customers.

QUESTION:
What is the difference between a Customer and a Consumer?

A customer is someone who buys the product.
A consumer is someone who consumes the product but does not necessarily buy it.

Take Dog food. Dogs don't care what the packaging or the colour of meat is like. You have to attract the Customer in this case.

Satisfaction comes in different forms within the Marketing mix.

If you are a **Manufacturer** selling to wholesale dealers then you need to make life easy for them to sell to **their** customers.
This is not just about your wonderful product or service in this scenario; it's more about selling **through** rather than selling **to.**

Have you got decent point of sale material, leaflets, shelf talkers etc. Maybe a display stand.
Will you consider employing a Manufacturers Sales Representative or Sales Agent?

How are your products packaged? Will they be seen easily?
Are the profit margins good for both Wholesale & Retail?
Do you need to address the Wholesale Sales Representatives?
Do you need to organise regular journey cycles?

IF you are a **Wholesaler** selling to **Retail**
Have you set your Rec. Retail price?
Have you researched the profit margins expected of the Retailer?
Are you prepared to offer local advertising?
Will you be having a team of Sales Representatives or Agents?
Will they need Product Knowledge and/or Sales Training?
Will you consider Business to business Mail order?
(A small list of Mail order Brokers is on page 36).

Selling Direct to the end user? How will you communicate?

Mail Order? Website? Social Media? Newspaper/Magazine Advertising?

Tele-sales?

As you can see we have just tipped the iceberg with much more to get through before you can see yourself being an established player in the market place.

12

We will now delve deeper into satisfying our clients by making sure we have covered some of the important aspects required to achieve a successful sale.

Make Selling Easy
Once you have got those first two elements of anticipate and identify sorted out you will find it easier to **satisfy** your customer requirements because you correctly anticipated and identified them.

The **satisfying** bit takes place during the actual sales presentation by putting across the relevant features and benefits. The whole selling (satisfying) process needs to be a properly structured one that is put across in a professional manner either face to face or remotely. I have run a number of Telesales training programs as well as face-to-face selling seminars and if you need that professional training then you can choose from one of my distance learning programs or an In-house company version. Once sold, the customer needs to feel good and happy and not bruised with the heavy-handed selling attitude that really does not do any favours at all for your business. You will find when checking out various sales training programs there is a section about "overcoming objections". Whilst that sounds sensible, my view is that if you, as a business person, have correctly anticipated and identified your customer requirements, **you will not have any objections!**

Chapter 5 – Face to face Selling

I was a guest speaker at a Trade Fair and I was to follow a number of Speakers who, in my view, were relying on the technical support of lots of slides using Power-Point.

The lights were dimmed and I could sense people getting bored and tired of yet another lengthy presentation.

Then it was my turn. I actually saw one delegate asleep in his chair!

I turned the lights on – walked onto the stage with a flipchart and easel and shouted "**Wake up**!!" Decidedly embarrassed they awoke from their bored stupor and I had their attention.

On the flipchart was one word - **SELL.**

However, I had stuck the two "Ls" with low tack tape onto the chart.

I then took off the "Ls" and turned them round so that the corners of each "L" joined together to form an "X". **Boy did I have their attention!**

Here is a small extract from my presentation.

> *In the nicest way – selling is like sex – a romance between two people.*
>
> *There is the **anticipation**. Both parties on their own making themselves look attractive. Looking good, smelling nice, groomed well.*
>
> *They both by chance attend the same dance hall / social club .*
>
> *He looks around with a view to **identify** a likely prospect. She too is doing the same thing. Their eyes meet momentarily but enough for recognition to take place. He looks again and their eyes once again meet, this time for a longer period. He smiles and she does in return.*
>
> *He decides to get up and walk towards her table and asks politely. "Do you mind if I join you?" She agrees and they start a conversation. She likes him because she feels that he has a genuine interest in her.*
>
> *The relationship builds, the features and benefits are presented and accepted and he subsequently **satisfies** her requirements **profitably.***

A very simplistic analogy that hit home to the audience because I didn't blind them with science and I presented a situation that most of them were able to relate to. In this next chapter you will find some tips to help you with your conversation with your prospect clients.

Please remember. We have two nasal passages, two ears, two eyes but only one mouth. It is therefore twice as important for us to smell, look and LISTEN than to talk.

We learn everything we know by smelling, looking and listening.

We learn nothing by talking.

Chapter 6 – Open Questions

> *"I have six good serving men who taught me all I knew.*
> *Their names were*
> *What? &*
> *Where? &*
> *When? &*
> *How? &*
> *Why? &*
> *Who?".*

These are known as "Open Questions" because they open up a dialogue.
What this means is that if you start a question with one of the above-mentioned words you will not receive a yes or no answer.

Such words are often used in interviewing techniques to get the recipient to open up with some information. You need to be natural about this otherwise it becomes an interrogation. Blend open questions with closed questions. Closed questions start with words like

Did it? Is it? Have you? Can you? Will you? Was it?

These words that start a question just seek confirmation of a Yes or No.

The attitude towards your prospect must be genuine and friendly.

WARNING;

Never speak badly of others, however bad they may really be. You never know they may be related to your prospect. If your prospect leads you on, plead ignorance and never voice your opinion good or bad because you're sure to be wrong on both counts.

I strongly recommend you read "How to win friends and influence people" by Dale Carnegie. It's a great book and it works.

Chapter 7 – Customer Requirements

Customer Care
The quality of communication between retailer and customer nowadays, in many cases, in my view, is quite deplorable. Customers should be used to being served in a very polite and respectful manner. Sadly, we get almost the opposite in a number of cases

Shop Assistants talking to each other whilst serving customers.

Proprietors of retail shops standing outside the fronts of their shops with their arms folded. That's sure to bring the Punters in!!

Assistants actually eating whilst serving!

Staff saying what they have been trained to say but you can tell that they really don't mean it. The electronic robotic answers that you get on the telephone is often much nicer than the human being – **Why??**

I have successfully helped retailers increase their bottom line without their having to spend a single extra penny on stock, or shop design, or better equipment. Purely done by following my Customer Care regime.

What was strange is they really didn't think that they were doing anything wrong? Please don't allow your business to fall into this trap.

I always use the formula that you need to treat every one of your customers as if each of them **was your very first customer.**

If you're on the phone ***Dial a smile - don't phone a groan!***
Believe me. People buy people and if you are providing a top-quality service, people will be prepared to pay that little bit more knowing that they are well looked after.
Please remember that when you are in a face-to-face situation you are a performer. The spotlight is on you. Be well-dressed, well

groomed, smell nice, no bad breath and double check before you go out with someone who knows you well. Nothing like old smelly garlic coming out of the pores of your skin in your customer's office.

If you look good – you will feel good and you will act good.

Be Yourself

I clearly recall in the late 60s working as a Sales Representative for a company selling Cigarettes. My patch was the East End and West End of London. In those days there was a marked difference in the class of people in each sector.
As I was brought up in the heart of East London playing on bombsites and having fun throwing stones at one another, I could pretty well handle myself with the local people there.

The company that I worked for had the sole agency in the UK for a number of different types of cigarettes that came from different parts of the world. Namely Disque Blue; Gitanes; Nazionale; Irish Cigarettes and American cigarettes such as Kent and Marlborough.

Covering East London was mostly Irish cigarettes and possibly some American. The West End was very cosmopolitan that covered the whole range that was on offer.

As I was representing a sole agency, I called upon the biggest wholesalers and major accounts who would buy in at up to the best rate of 50,000 cigarettes.

Calling upon the East London punters, you need to know that a conversation could not take place without uttering the "F" word in nearly every sentence. I was used to that so it wasn't difficult for me to stand up to a major buyer of a group of Pubs who, was of a very large stature with a loud voice to go with it.

We hit it off very well because I believe I stood up to him when he would swear his head off saying how expensive the rate was. I in turn would speak the only language that he could understand and found myself speaking out as loud as he was.

I firmly believe that he was quite amused at the way I retaliated and on a regular weekly basis he and I would go through this play-acting, quite to his satisfaction.

Having obtained my 50,000 cigarettes order from him, I would then be off to the West End Soho area calling on the Playboy Club as well as various Cigar Shops.

Then to Kensington where I would meet a very posh lady buyer from the West Kensington Hotel. She would offer me a seat and we would share tea and biscuits whilst she went through her cigarette order.

Our conversation was very different to the East London area. I managed to adapt to a more aristocratic style of speech without once uttering the "F" word. Here again, I built up a very nice business relationship.

At a subsequent sales meeting I was approached by my Sales Manager who told me that there was to be a new Irish Cigarette that was going to be launched in Dublin. He said that it would be wise to invite all the major clients to Dublin on company expenditure and that I would be the Key Accounts Manager looking after my clients.

This, for me, was a great opportunity to visit Ireland and enjoy a new-found environment all on the company expenditure.

The afternoon had arrived and the launch took place with all the benefits
being presented for this new cigarette. It was a great success for PR.

"David!" shouted my Sales Manager from the other side of a very large stately room. "Come here! There are two of your customers who cannot stop singing your praises!"

Well you can guess who they were. Boy did I have to think quickly!

I managed to prise away the West End buyer for a quick quiet chat out of earshot. I offered her a drink and excused myself to talk to the East End Guy in the manner that he was used to. To this day, I don't know how I got away with it. Big mistake and that moment still haunts me today!

Be adaptable but **BE YOURSELF**

It's your business! You can do what you like when you like.

Some of you may be starting a business having had a background of working for someone else who ran a successful business of their own, or, you worked for a large company that had strict rules and regulations about how they went about their business.

Naturally you are now able to do what you want to do.
You can stay in bed all day if you want!

I suggest you pretend that you are still working for that large company. Impose some rules upon yourself.

If you operate from home then go into your "office" with a label on the door that says "Office" and leave your domestic baggage outside the door.

Chapter 8 – Profitably

Turnover is Vanity - Profit is Sanity
You are in business to make a profit and you have a bottom line that you must stick to. Never say to a client that you will not reduce your price. Better to say that you **can't.** The art of negotiation comes into play here and you may be selling a product that attracts high profit margins with a wide negotiating area to play with. Use it wisely and don't be to eager to get too low too early. All part of the selling process. I often wonder how some business people continue to kid themselves when spouting about their annual turnover being say 3 or 4 million, only to find that their company expenditure exceeded the turnover and I am called in to rectify the situation. Do you know what your Gross profit is before tax? Do you know your net profit after tax and expenditure? Get yourself a nice easy piece of software that works it all out for you.

If you do have a product or service that provides you with a sizeable profit then please ensure that you have indelibly printed in your mind your lowest acceptable price that still gives you a decent margin. And never go below it.

Chapter 9 – Getting there and staying there

Nothing in this materialistic world that we live in lasts forever. Not even your product or service. There are phases and cycles that alter the whole aspect of how we deliver our products and services to constantly **satisfy** our customers.

The Boston Matrix is an excellent guideline to follow when it comes to product life cycle. The word "cycle" is very appropriate because fashions and other time-based products and services do come back, possibly in a different kind of package. You just need to be ahead of the game in readiness to make any necessary changes.

The Wild Card

My simplistic approach to the Boston Matrix is for you to imagine that your business is an Aeroplane ready to take off. It's brand new and nobody has flown it ever before. As such it is "A Wild Card".

Much time and effort has been spent manufacturing this aircraft with every attention to ensure that it has met all the required safety regulations. That done, the Pilot, who also needs to be qualified, is ready to take all his passengers (customers) to their destination.

The Aeroplane accelerates down the runway ready to take off. In a matter of seconds it actually leaves the ground. This big chunk of metal full of passengers and baggage manages to defy gravity and leaves the ground. The amount of fuel (money, advertising, promotion) is quite substantial at this early stage particularly as it is a new craft that has never flown before.

Launching a business is much like this Aeroplane. Much research and strategic marketing activity all has to be put together before you even expose your product or service to the market place.

Even if you are going at a reduced risk of launching an existing product into an existing market place you still have to be sure that you are not going to have an empty plane if you have not calculated your best profitable ticket price that is competitive enough to attract passengers.

Looking positively, the aeroplane continues to climb at a fascinating incline and slowly begins to level out.

We are now about to go to the second stage of your product's life cycle.

The Rising Star

No coughs or engine splutters. Everyone on board sighs with great relief. Everything that was planned ended up being correct and the aeroplane continues to climb to a level of 40,000 ft. in readiness for its long haul to a faraway country.

Less fuel is being used, less pressure on the craft and pilot Everyone is happy. A lot of other aeronautical companies are looking at this new craft with some envy as they see this as a possible threat. The aeroplane took off more quietly. It is a smoother take off than its rivals. It has some features that have been more beneficial to the passengers. There is even more legroom for people to be more comfortable during their flight.

All in all, so far, a great success. Pilot and company directors and owners are very pleased with all the work and effort so far. As a result of so many people seeing the take off, more bookings are coming in for further flights.

The plane has just reached 40,000 ft and is levelling off.

The Rising Star has risen as is seamlessly moving into the next category.

The Cash Cow

You've made it! You are all moving at a nice quiet horizontal flight using minimal fuel and flying easily at 400 miles per hour. There are quite a few hours yet to go, but the aircraft and pilot feel that they could carry on forever.

WARNING – Nothing lasts forever!

Along the journey the pilot has been told that he will be going towards a country that has recently been involved with an international disagreement which has resulted in the aircraft having to make a detour as the country concerned will not allow this plane into their airspace.

The pilot has full control of the aircraft and has to make a decision quickly. The detour is calculated and an additional 200 miles needs to be covered before getting back to the original flight path. The pilot realises that there will not be sufficient fuel to cover the full journey.

Communication takes place with various air flight control centres at other countries where the plane has had to detour. Two of the four control centres are contacted and refuse to allow the plane to land

If the plane is not allowed to land anywhere it will crash with the pilot and all the passengers in it. Should that happen it will no longer function and like any product or service that is no longer viable it becomes ….

A Dead Dog

Your product or service may have a life cycle of quite a few years. Much depends upon a number of factors, mainly how the competition reacts to your presence. How you react to the competition and the changes in customer requirements.

If the plane crashes then there will be no confidence in any future passengers wanting to go aboard that type of aircraft. Those that book will cancel and be happy to lose their deposits.

The third flight control centre also refuses to allow the plane to land.

Thankfully, because of an SOS message the fourth flight control centre allows the plane to land upon the runway for refuelling.

Although you are grounded as a dead dog not being able to go anywhere, the re-fuelling process is a process of change which allows the aircraft to continue upon its way.

Once arriving at its destination, work is carried out to maximise the fuel tank's capacity to enable the return flight to take place without any undue disturbance.

With a new fuel tank and other modifications it is once again a **Wild Card** which will, no doubt,

become a **Rising Star** and then a **Cash Cow** where your product and service would like to be for a very long time.

Look upon the Boston Matrix alongside Ansoff's theory.

The bigger the risk the longer you will be a wild card

Always be aware of your competition and remember that when you reach the **Cash Cow** stage, that is where every one of your competitors wish to be. They want to be where you are. Brand leadership is a great thing but can come at a cost.

I was involved with a small team of Regional Managers launching a product called Arrid Extra Dry. It was a great product and unit sales sold exceptionally well. A lot of money was spent on advertising to get the product to brand leader. It succeeded in attaining that position, but at great cost. Whilst the product continued to be distributed via wholesalers into the market place, most of the sales force, including myself, were made redundant and some serious surgery had to take place to turn the losses back into profit.

This type of tweaking had to be done otherwise Arrid would have immediately become a dead dog never to be seen again.

Whether you are a large or small concern the rule of thumb is the same.

As you progress with your product life cycle, it is of paramount importance that you constantly keep up to date with what is happening within your market sector.

Read all the relevant magazines, newspapers. Try and go to trade shows. Failing that, find out who are exhibiting and check out their websites etc.

The more you know about your competition the stronger you will be.

If you are just starting up you have a wonderful opportunity of doing so for surprisingly little money.

The internet global platform is now accessible by having a very simple inexpensive website.

There are numerous ways of producing a site for yourself. One of the most popular is "Wordpress". They have made life so easy for anyone to make a good start.

For those who need some hand-holding in a step-by- step fashion. There is a set of 2 DVDs that is specifically for beginners. You can find information on these as well as other business educational DVDs at

www.davidfentonpublishing.co.uk

More about websites in Chapter 13

Chapter 10 – The S.W.O.T analysis

S.W.O.T. stands for Strengths, Weaknesses, Opportunities and Threats

In my view businesses owners are the world's worst judges to make a list under each of the above-mentioned headings.

Let's take a look at each element;

Strengths

This is an opportunity for a business owner, directors and management to sit down and blow their own trumpets about how much better they are against the competition. If there are genuine areas that support this then let that trumpet sing and write down all of those strengths as a means of reference the next time a SWOT is carried out.

Weaknesses

Business Owners and Managers really do need to expect to take things on the chin without getting emotional.

Could it be the management style of a particular individual that is causing a weakness within the organisation?

Could it be that there is a poor customer care system or **no** customer care system in place?

What about the Receptionist? Does he or she politely receive people?

What about your telephone techniques and skills?

There are more weaknesses that will appear on the horizon if you speak to the right people – The Cleaner, The Window Cleaner, The Postman, The Cook, The Customer and anyone that the Management come into contact with commercially.

Opportunities

Opportunities for new products or services could become "Wild Cards" (See Boston Matrix – chapter 9).

You may have a "Dead Dog" on your hands that may require replacing.

There may be a legal opportunity that could trigger a special promotion.

Perhaps a forthcoming acquisition could be on the cards.

SWOT meetings providing this kind of creativity from previous research is always very healthy and could end up being one of the major strengths.

Threats

Competition in itself is a permanent threat. Sensible research into the market place to establish what market share the company has and what direction it is going is always important to look at regularly, no less that once a month.

A competitor may have a special offer coming up. How will this affect your sales? What are you going to do about it?

A SWOT meeting should comprise key Managers and/or Directors and heads of departments if a medium to large company. A start-up or small business will need the owners or partners to be present alongside an outside person who has had dealings with the company.

Situations change quite quickly and so I urge you to make these meetings once a month.

Chapter 11 Secrets of Successful Advertising

<u>How to get Customers and keep them</u>

The first rule of thumb here is to make sure that whatever product or service you have to offer, you must be sure that you have a "hungry crowd" of prospects willing to buy.

Your task now is to find those people.

" Yeah ! O.K. Dave what do you expect me to do? - put a sandwich board on and stroll up and down the road advertising it?".

Answer? Yes you could, and it might have the desired effect if you, at the same time give out flyers to those who have approached you.

Let us assume you don't really want to do that. After all, this is all about earning money from the comfort of your own home, so let's see if we can keep it that way. Here are some options depending upon your budget.

Advertise in Local, Regional or National Newspapers.

Local neatly printed Postcards in Newsagents shops.

Leaflets that go into free delivered local Newspapers.

Appoint leaflet distributors to carry out leaflet drops for you.

Produce a website (Session 4).

Produce a Blog (Session 4)

Posters that are strategically positioned to attract the targeted prospects.

Obtain details of businesses from trade journals and local councils.

Purchase prospect lists from list brokers (session 3).

Join various internet forums

Join a local trade forum

Join a local Chamber of Trade.

Sell on Ebay (session 6)

Consider Google Adwords as a kick start. (session 4)

Wherever possible, include a simple form for prospects to enter their contact details. When they become true clients of yours you then need to keep their details for any follow up offers etc.

By persevering with one or more of the above methods, you can build up a database which you can then use as a basis for your first means of direct contact.

As you can see advertising can come in many forms so it is vital that you advertise your product or service in the right type of media at the right time. Here again so many of my clients fall down by just doing a scatter gun type approach. If you are targeting over 60s try Saga type Mags. as opposed to a Magazine that is of a more general nature. Before you advertise, research what the readership is and the general age group etc. who buy the Magazine.

Keeping your customers

Any customer of yours represents a strong contribution towards your livelihood. Keep them up to date. Offer them new and exciting fresh offers and information. Make a friend of them. They will become your eager forms of recommendation to others.

Above all look after your customers and give them honest and reliable service. If you are ever wrong. Accept it and compensate your customers that they see you as a very fair and honourable person. There will always be a small percentage of clients who take advantage of what you have to offer for free etc. and never buy from you. Thankfully, there are also many more who are genuine and will help you if they have received the service that they expect.

You will find that as you build up your reputation (Moving into the Rising Star sector) you will have clients asking you for information etc. which they will happily pay for, because they want to deal with you.

Building your database is time consuming and although you may be itching to get your product off the ground, don't let it take off like an empty aeroplane.

The object of an aeroplane is to transport its passengers from one point to another. If you have no targeted interested customers you could be just like the empty aeroplane. Taking off to its destination with just the pilot and its crew (You) getting to its destination but not completely fulfilling its objective. To be profitable. (Definition of Marketing chapter 1).

Formulating your advert or Mailshot is very important.

Use the tried and tested formula adopted by all the great Marketing professionals :- **A.I.D.A.**

A.I.D.A.

Here is the process you need to use for any product or service when you structure the wording for any Mailshot or Advert or Website

A.I.D.A. - One of the great Marketing principles often forgotten.

Attention

Interest

Desire

Action

Attention

You really need to firstly grab the prospects' attention in just a few words. They have to be catchy and intriguing to arouse curiosity.

So, if you are selling Golf Balls - something like ….

"Hole in one Golf Balls - Every time? "

Notice the question mark. You can then be friendly and continue with an initial phrase that discounts the questioning statement and move slowly on to the next element. All you are doing here is Grabbing Attention!

You could spend an awful long time working on just half a dozen words but, believe me, time well spent. If you don't grab their attention, they will not read on and it goes straight in the bin.

We then slide into the second element

Interest

You have grabbed their attention and aroused their curiosity.

That curiosity must not die. You have to ensure that whatever they read next is exciting enough to arouse their interest.

The important things to write are to provide and feed out one or two benefits of what you are selling. Too many times, I have found some adverts so boring because of an overload of information.

Remember you should be advertising to a targeted interested prospect, previously screened as being someone who has an interest in the type of stuff you sell anyway!

You really need to build up benefits and understand the difference between benefits and features.

Features are what it's got

Benefits are what it does for you.

Which do you think is going to be more interesting to the prospect? Exactly **BENEFITS BENEFITS BENEFITS.**

For example, if you are marketing a 9.5Gb DVD and said to someone who knows nothing about computers etc.

" This is a 9.5gb DVD". It means NOTHING to them.

If on the other hand you say "This 9.5gb DVD will enable you to record two full scale feature films lasting over 5 hours".

You are talking the language they understand.

Make sure your Mailshots contain these gems.

Now by this time they are interested but how many times have you received a Mailshot and you read it right to the end and say to yourself "Mmm that's interesting - I will put that away in the file and get back to it because I might take that up some day." Some day huh! Never, more likely!

That's because only the first two elements were used in the structure Attention & Interest. You have to generate the Interest to such a degree it gets the prospect to a level of desire ....

Desire

Let's just analyse the difference between Interest and desire.

Interest is a level-headed attitude to something that has captured your attention.

Desire, on the other hand, is so strong that it can break the rules of logic and common sense. Imagine this being said ....

"Oh! darling I know the House is £15,000 more than what we budgeted for but I want it." There you go, desire at its best.

The prospect has got to stage of yearning for the product or service. Their emotions are running high for it. They are "sold" on it.

So what do we do on an advert to get them from interest to desire?

You need to feed out a nice juicy Carrot! A freebie gift -

A special bonus. A never again repeatable, one off opportunity. A promise of a price rise in the not too distant future. Extra hours etc. etc.

Here, once again, too many marketers kill the interest by following it up with garbage of features and information that really doesn't make them excited at all.

Be enthusiastic. Show your enthusiasm in the written word.

Use the words, Fantastic! Exclusive! Much sought after! Rare! Unique! Unbeatable! etc.

At this stage your prospect is going to become a little impatient in wanting to know the price and possibly placing an order with you. Give them what they want but give them more than what they want to really close the deal.

Once your prospect has got to this stage it should be very easy to slide into the next element.

Action

Assuming your prospect has now got to the stage of desire, you need to satisfy that desire by making a seamless journey to the action stage where they complete the direct debit details or send you a cheque etc.

A simple form with a "Freepost" address arrangement usually works well. You only pay the return postage when it's been posted to you and those that have been posted to you will mostly be new customers.

Magazines

Look out for specialist magazines that relate to the types of products or information you have to offer.

Once again you need to match up your product to someone who has a genuine interest.

Go to your Newsagents and take a good look at some of the Magazines on the shelf. Buy a few, if you can and take a good look at any special features and offers that the editors are publicising.

Check out the advertising rates.

There are many thousands of Magazines that are read cover to cover that are never seen in shops. These are subscribed magazines purchased by very keenly interested readers who have a passion for that sport or hobby or interest etc.

Circulation is lower than the high street magazines but the readership levels are much higher.

Here you will get a much better advertising rate deal and the opportunity of some editorial. This can be a much more cost-effective form of advertising. Take a look at this website that shows you a search opportunity of virtually any specialist subject magazine that is currently on the market with all the necessary contact details.

www.mediauk.com

You will see four tabs at the top. Click on Magazines and away you go.

Newspapers

Local, Regional, or National. Your choice.

You need to be clear of your objective.

If you are selling and wishing to make your transaction on a website that you have produced, do not waste your money giving out all the info in a newspaper advert. A National classified box type advert in say the Telegraph could set you back a couple of hundred pounds.

If you wish to direct readers to your website you need to use A.I.D.A.

and come up with no more than about three to four lines on a lineage advert that will cost less than a hundred pounds and that will be just as effective.

Affiliation

Here is an opportunity for you to use your database of interested prospects to sell to them products by acting as a commission agent or affiliate for a company that is already actively involved in producing the product or item. Such organisations generally offer very good commissions to help expand their business (as I do - see session 10).

Let's take a look at two of the most popular websites that engage such activity.

1) **Clickbank**

This company specialises in the publicity of products and services that are readily available in a digital format such as an E-Book that the recipient can download onto their computer and then either read it off or print it off and use as a hard copy.

All you need to do is visit www.clickbank.com

Click on the tab "Promote products" and follow the "sign on" instructions.

You will then be able to associate yourself with a whole variety of products that you can promote.

If, whoever you have contacted buys from your click bank merchant, you will automatically receive a commission for that purchase.

There are many people making a very good living just by doing this.

The secret here is to

- Look up click bank merchants and check out the various products.
- Google up a search list against those products to find level of interest.
- Once found, register with clickbank and obtain the link that you need.
- Use either your own database or one purchased from a list broker.
- Send out mail shots, emails etc. to those prospects with the link.

I know of someone who carried out this process religiously and knuckled down to doing one product a day up to 5 products a week. In a year with over 200 products, mostly niche products he ended up making a very nice living without buying any stock. His money was just spent on buying in prospect lists and sending them out by mail or Email.

TIP:- Usually because of the downloadable nature of this kind of activity most products sell at a low priced rate. Products selling at just under the £20 mark usually go well. Remember that click bank have everything in dollars so you need to convert to get the UK sterling equivalent price.

2) **Paydotcom**

This company works very much the same way as clickbank but gets involved with physical products as well as digital products.

This opens up the market place and gives you a greater opportunity to earn more money as an affiliate. There is no reason why you cannot use both organisations. Just sign up and follow the online instructions.

Go to:- www.paydotcom.com

Paydotcom accept and use paypal as a means of transaction which is an excellent process. I strongly recommend you to open up a paypal account as this will also be put to good use when selling on Ebay

3) Third part websites.

This is where you can really get sucked into the hype of organisations offering you a complete turnkey package including a website etc. where you don't need any selling skills because its all been done for you.

Well the website is done for you.

The products are there for you

The payment mechanism is done for you.

But where are the customers?

Oh you can buy that as an extra can you? That goes directly into their massive global database?

Or maybe they do not have a customer finding facility.

Sure you can put that website into the google search engine regime, but that website will be much the same as all the other websites that they are selling to other "dying to make few bob" customers who are definitely not going to get hundreds and hundreds of hungry people wanting the product unless a lot more money is thrown at it to get your website up into a top ranking level worthy of being seen on the first page of a Google list.

Hang on! This is not always the case. There are some that are very good.

However, to really begin to earn money you need to build your own database and use that knowing who the website is going to be visited by.

You can then follow it up on Email without being accused of spamming.

Once again, look very carefully at the product range offered. Check how competitive they are. If they are not competitive you could end up buying a year's subscription for this great all singing dancing website. Get loads of clicks and visits, but no sales.

TIP: Affiliation is a great way to start earning money. Your method of advertising has to be accurately targeted.

Ensure you work only to your affordable budget. Negotiate heavily on advertising rates with subscribed magazines fairly close to their copy closing day. You will be pleasantly surprised.

Chapter 12 - Getting the most out of your mailshots

Besides contacting potential clients via Email, you also have the opportunity of corresponding with them by sending them a Mailshot in the post.

To really get the most of offline activity you need to have a list of potential clients clearly targeted. This as you can guess takes us straight back to our first session where you will need to carry out some research.

There are many List Brokers who will allow you to rent lists of targeted prospects. At the end of this session there is a list of List Brokers that you may find useful.

If the List Brokers have done their jobs properly you should receive from them an up to date list of targeted prospects in an area of your choice. Prices vary and you need to get to understand that generally from the Brokers you really do get what you pay for. Higher price, generally higher quality.

You would also receive them in the format of your choice.

Let us now assume that you have your list of prospects and you are ready to produce your Mailshot. I have found two successful ways of doing this.

The Postcard Mailshot.

You can order Coloured Picture Postcards customised to suit your requirements and printed to your specification.

www.vistaprint.com is a firm that I recommend as I have found their service and quality excellent and prices very reasonable.

The beauty of the Card is that it is instantly read, even by the Postman. Do make sure you have something that links one side of the card to the other, just in case it drops on the doormat wrong side up.

You can easily Merge your addresses on a database and then adjust the sliders on your Printer to take the correct size and away you go.

The A4 Sheet flyer

This is the most popular type of Mail shot that is sent out in pre - addressed envelopes. Again some printers will print envelopes as well as paper.

The other way is to mail merge the addresses on your A4 sheet of paper and position the address details to coincide with a Window Envelope.

Mailshots based upon traditional Mail order offline methods, if targeted correctly, can be very successful.

If you can include a DVD with your Mail shot you arouse the curiosity even more so and you can expect more prospects at least watching/listening before it finds its way into the bin as opposed to it going in the bin before its even looked at.

Whatever you use, make sure you use it for the right purpose. If you want your prospect to go to the Computer and look up your website then just feed out a few great benefits of your offer just like feeding out a small amount of bait to catch a fish. Too much information - No good at all!!

Arouse the curiosity. Focus clearly upon your objective. Ask yourself. What do I want this Mail shot to do?

Mailshot Conversion Ratios

I always believe in keeping things simple and I have no wish to blind you with science. Let us refer to the Mailshot Conversion Ratio as MCR. The MCR is just a fraction.

It represents the number of prospects that bought from you or gave you a positive response divided by the number of Mail shots you sent out.

Invariably the average MCR seems to settle around the 1.5% or 2% mark for targeted prospects. However, this could be much higher for really specialised niche markets.

When you do Mailshots you need to cost things out properly before you spend away all your money.

Cost of Printing

Cost of Paper or Postcards

Cost of Envelopes

Cost of Postage

Let's say you sent out 1,000 highly targeted A4 Mailshots with a view of an instant sale from your website of £60

Cost of printing 1,000 A4 Paper	say £55
Cost of A4 Paper	say £10
Cost of Envelopes	say £20
Cost of postage @ 57p each	= £570
(discounted postal charges – see chapter 12)	
Total Cost	£655

With a 2% return on your mail shots you will

Receive 20 orders each of £60 = £1200

You will make a profit of £545.00

Now if your product is sold too cheaply. Say £30

You still get 20 orders totalling £600.00

You will make a loss of £55.

This is because your fixed costs are the same.

Lower your price and you substantially lower your profits.

44

I have known people rub their hands with glee when they get some positive orders coming in only to find that in reality they made a loss. All that effort for nothing.

There is a fantastic saying that has always kept with me throughout my business life. This was touched on in Chapter 8.

"Turnover is Vanity"

"Profit is Sanity"

Check your costs before you get really emotionally involved in convincing yourself that you have got the greatest thing since sliced bread.

Mailshot Timing

Did you know that by following up a Mailshot that you have sent out you DOUBLE your chances of converting prospects into real business customers?

If you have Telephone Number details as well as addresses then you have a wonderful opportunity of following up what you have sent out.

Timing is of the essence here.

So many businesses lose out on conversions simply because they opt for 2nd class post. Why?

If you send out a Mailshot by 2nd class Post it could take up to 5 days to get to the recipient.

Now, I said -up to 5 days.

When do they receive it? Next day? 2 days later? 3 days later? You just don't know.

Now an over-eager person decides to follow up the Mailshot after say 3 days only to find the person on the other end of the phone hasn't even received it yet. Another wasted phone-call.

OK let's follow it up after 6 days shall we?

By that time the recipient has had so many other things to think about you are going to find it really tough trying to explain exactly what it was they supposed to have received.

First Class Post is generally received 98% of the time the following working day.

Here you wait two working days and then follow up.

If you send out on Friday, expect them to receive it on Monday and follows up on Tuesday.

Believe me it's worth the extra expense because you will get a much more positive response on the phone.

If you are not going to follow up the Mailshot, as is the case where you are just directing them to your Website that is going to act as the closing process of the deal, then 2nd class post is just fine.

Offline and other traditional offline forms of advertising should always be considered in conjunction with your online activities.

Newspaper advertising etc. directing readers to your website is always worth pursuing. Obviously much relates to costs and you have to work according to your budget.

Targeted Mailshots, for me, have always shown fairly good results.

It is also beneficial for you to purchase lists from list brokers for multiple use. It is quite extraordinary that you can send the same Mailshot out to the same list 2 or even 3 times and still get a steady 1% or 2% response every time.

Some List Brokers

www.Marketingfile.com

www.Hillitedms.co.uk

www.whichlist.com

www.Tlsdata.co.uk

There are more and you can google up "List Brokers" and search around for the best deal for you.

Chapter 13 - Cut Price Postage

Have a look at the mail that comes into your home and you will find that quite a lot of the larger companies have a "Mailsort" logo on the Envelope. This is where the sender uses a fulfilment house to send out all the mail.

By doing so there is also a saving on postage because the fulfilment house receives the mail in strict postcode form which actually does half the work that the post office sorting office does. By doing so the post office provide a discount off the postage for bulk mailing.

You may think that you have to purchase millions of mailings etc to do this but this is not the case.

I believe that the minimum rate is 1,000 A4 large envelopes and 3,000 standard envelopes for a mail sort operation to take place.

Depending on what fulfilment house you use, you may well be able to send them (in postcode form) 3,000 standard envelopes printed up with the addresses together with two or three inserts to keep within the 100gm minimum standard postage rate.

If you work it well you could find that the discount from postage makes a big contribution towards the payment of the fulfilment process.

If you google up "Fulfilment houses U.K." you will get a host of companies offering you their services.

Chapter 14 – Selling at Exhibitions

Selling at Exhibitions can be a very lucrative way of obtaining fresh business and bringing new products or services to your existing clients.

National Exhibitions that promote certain Market sectors at venues like the NEC give you the opportunity to boldly find out a lot more about your competition and vice versa.

Such "shell-like" stands are not cheap and you really need to plan thoroughly about this particular form of promotion as a separate unique campaign.

If this is to be your first time, I suggest that you first go and attend such an exhibition as a Visitor. You can easily glean more about your competitors without putting all your cards on the table.

If your business involves being a sales agent for manufacturers then you have a great opportunity of picking out potential suppliers to boost your commission.

You will be amazed at the number of Exhibitors who openly advertise "Agents required" on their stands.

Once you have acquainted yourself with the environment, you can then decide whether or not it will be viable to attend as an Exhibitor.

Your next task is to check your overall costs applicable to an Exhibition to include your time away from the Office as well as possible staff. Your fuel and overnight expenditure where applicable. Your stock and stationery requirements.

All these plus the overall cost of the space that you will be renting. Generally, a shell scheme offers a choice of sizes which include a front facia board. Optional extras such as carpeting etc. will be shown on your price list/application form.

Many exhibitors look at the overall cost of such an exhibition and project that cost for 12 months of business originating from the show.

For example, you may have a new client that gives you an order at the Exhibition and thereafter regular monthly business. The important thing to consider is that you must be prepared to be able to afford for a complete flop where little or no business, for no particular reason, causes a loss.

Assuming you are going, let's move onto colour schemes.

The most striking colours are Blue with Yellow. If you have your own Logo then that too can be applied to the facia.

Think about doing an Exhibition offer to attract new leads.

When I invented my "NEK-PAK" (chapter 2) we exhibited at a Promotional Exhibition and brought quite a lot of stock of the product in different colours and one in every 10 packs had a £5 note inside. You couldn't see inside the packs being coloured and opaque. We sold each pack at a special offer of £2 and as soon as someone had found a fiver, we began to get a queue of people wanting to buy. We sold 200 packs for an income of £400 with a giveaway of 20 x £5 notes giving us a net profit of £300. We sold out and could have sold more. That went a good way to pay for our stand. Think outside the box to pull in the crowd.

Getting an audience

If you have a product that you can demonstrate you are halfway there.

Get yourself ready and when you see some passing traffic just get on with your demonstration without the eye contact but make sure they can hear you.

They, if interested, will stop and look at what you are doing. You can then glance in their direction and smile whilst you continue

with your demonstration. Your demo is a Sales presentation offering the benefits of the product and you need to close the sale by offering them a special exhibition offer. You then just go into a loop and re-start the demo as others may have just missed it and will hang on. Give time for people to ask questions. If they are interested then it is for you to convert that interest to **desire** (AIDA Chapter 11).

If you are not doing a demo then whenever you see someone passing by you need to speak to them with an open question (Chapter 6).

For example, if you are selling central hesating, an opening line would be

"Hello Sir, What type of heating are you using at present? "

You are there to sell. Make every passer-by count. You have about 3 seconds only to make the approach.

Exhibition work for some companies has been the mainstay of their business. It could be yours.

Chapter 15 - **Producing a Website that really works for you**

Website production for many people is fraught with fear of having to be technically minded and/or having to be knowledgeable about the internet etc.

Nothing could be further from the truth if you are prepared to put a little time and effort into it.

There are many companies who use Website production firms who are producing websites everyday for a living.

Once you have become proficient at producing your own website there is really no reason why you cannot do the same yourself and have a website production business of your own.

Having good control of your website with the opportunity of maintaining your site easily is very important.

The first stage is to find a good "Host". Such organisations may charge for a "Domain name" and "Web space".

The situation is very competitive and you can get some very good hosting packages at very reasonable cost.

Before going into greater depth, I am going to take you through a flow chart type priority list so that you do things in the correct order.

1) Research some decent well-respected Hosting companies.

2) Decide upon your website domain name.

3) Decide how long you want it for

4) Buy web space for your website

5) Produce your website

6) Upload your site to the world wide web.

O.K. let's go through this list stage by stage ;-

1) **The research**

There are thousands of hosting companies available all jostling to provide you with the best deal. I have used www.uk2.net for some time now without any problems. They are not, in my view, the lowest priced but I do get value for money.

Everyday you will find some other company and with a little research just take the plunge and go for it.

However, you will not be able to sign up with anyone until you have decided upon a domain name for your site.

2) **Your Website domain name**

Any decent hosting company has a search option for you to complete.

You may have had an idea up your sleeve for a name and you put it in the search box only to find that someone else thought about the same thing.

It is therefore important that you give yourself a few different options.

Once you have been given confirmation of your name you can feel good and relax knowing that nobody else can have your name. It's unique to you.

3) How long do I have this name for?

Depending on the hosting company you can opt for different lengths of time before your domain name expires.

If you are just starting out and not really sure about whether or not your website is going to succeed or not, my recommendation is you opt for a three month period if you can.

This will give you sufficient time for various search engines to play their part.

You will also be able to allow the domain to expire without having had to commit yourself with too much money over a period of one or two years.

I have produced a variety of websites and found some worked better for me than others. It's a constant maintenance program really.

The important thing is the content and regular update of the site where necessary.

4) Buying Webspace

A good Hosting company will sell you web space and you can probably get a pretty good deal without paying out too much money.

Shop around and have a good look through what is available to you before deciding.

5) **Producing your website**.

Wow! Here is where one can open up a real big can of worms. Let's try and keep it simple shall we?

Firstly, I have been using a software for the past 10 years called

Serif Webplus 8. I suppose I should have replaced it by now but it has produced for me some really good websites and for around £50 you can today get a pretty good choice of software that will really make life very easy for you.

I can be quite frank with you and say that my own Technical knowledge of html language etc. is extremely limited.

All I want is something that is designed for internet idiots where I can just type in easily what I want and upload without any difficulty.

The Serif web plus 8 for me was the biz.

Writing this book, however, has prompted me to check out what is now available so that I can advise you by email what is currently sensible and easy to use. Watch this space!

Different software packages will have their own set of easy to follow instructions so it would be wrong for me to go through just my own at this stage.

Let us therefore assume that you have purchased your software and you are fully acquainted with the way you can use it.

The other option without having to buy any software is you go to a hosting company that has its own built in website production facility

5) **Getting Prospects to your Blog or Website**

There are a number of different ways you can attract visitors to your sites.

I will now provide you with a variety of different methods and ideas.

Depending on what you are offering you will choose which is most appropriate. Often more than one method proves fruitful.

A proper campaign within your budget is always the sensible approach.

6) Joint ventures

As you have a new Website and just starting up, you will find it useful to look at other websites that are marketing products in line with yours but not competing.

For example, if you are marketing "Left handed Golf Instruction" information

You could link up with someone who is involved in Marketing "Left handed Golf Clubs".

You find out who owns the website. Contact them by Email and suggest that you swap links or banners.

As your website is fresh with very few visitors and you joint venture with a website that has thousands of visitors then there is a pretty good chance that you will get some visitors from the other site.

Do that type of linking with 3 or 4 more websites, you could be in the money!

Chapter 16 - Offline advertising

Offline really means any kind of advertising that is not carried out on the internet.

Mail shots

Magazine adverts

Local Papers

National Papers

Radio

T.V.

Parish News

Leaflets in doors.

All of these with the correct (here we go again) - **A.I.D.A.** language will produce visitors for you.

Email

Sending Emails out to known targeted potential clients is another method. Please be aware of "spamming". This is a term that really means you are making an approach via the internet to an individual who has not fully agreed with the idea of your contacting them.

There is a fine line to be drawn here so to try and clarify the point.

If you ever complete a form for information or freebies you may well be asked to tick a box that says. *Will you agree to allow one of our respected associate companies to send information to you?* Or words to that effect.

If you did tick the box you have, in effect "Opted in" to allow communication to be made to you.

You can purchase bona fide "Opt in" lists of prospects from a variety of List Brokers who actually make a living renting out such lists of possible leads.

These vary from around 3p to 5p each on Email and about £120-£150 per thousand if you want to do a Mail shot.

Google up "List Brokers" and you will find a myriad of eager sellers.

4) **Offer Commission**

Offer commission and take on "Affiliates" to help sell your products for you.

You can have a www.paydotcom affiliate link so that anyone who goes to your website or paydotcom can become an affiliate. As an affiliate they, in turn will direct visitors to your site where you get business and subsequently pay commission to your agents.

Summary

Joint venture links

Offline contact - The list is by no means exhaustive.

Email - Beware of Spamming.

Commission - Employ Agents/Affiliates

If you have done you're A.I.D.A. correctly you will get a percentage of visitors buying from you.

The Action they take will be to make the purchase.

How are they going to do that?

By **Paypal**

If you haven't already done so I urge you to open up a Paypal account.

Paypal has proved to be an excellent worldwide method of receiving and sending money without any upfront costs.

They take a commission from the value of the sale.

Your visitors do not have to have a paypal account. They can pay via debit or credit cards through to paypal and you are therefore able to accept most well-known cards without having to pay annual charges.

Not everyone wants to pay via Paypal so you must also have a facility address where they can send you cheques.

Open up the Paypal account and go to www.paypal.co.uk

There you will find methods of putting in "Buy now" buttons on your website.

Paypal is also the main payment structure that is used for Ebay.

You are well advised therefore to get that underway before you complete your Websites.

Chapter 17 - Search Engine Optimisation

When producing your website or Blog you will need to ensure that all the necessary search engines that crawl around the big wide web are working to maximum effectiveness thus getting your site up and running when someone googles up a keyword that is relevant to your site content.

This does not create thousands of visitors overnight.

It is a slow process. Bear in mind you are not the only individual putting up a website. Thousands upon thousands are being exposed daily. You do have to be patient. It can take quite a few weeks or even months before you see any real results coming from it.

Your website should not be something that you look at and be impressed with if nobody else is visiting it.

Don't rely upon only one form of signposting.

Search Engines

Press adverts

Business Cards

Flyers

Word of Mouth

Mailshots

Leaflets

Html links

Online advertising

All play their part in signposting prospect visitors to your website or Blog.

You can even employ search engine optimisation specialists who for a fee will ensure that your site is always on page 1. Much depends upon your budget.

There is a great set of DVDs on SEO for you to carry out your own SEO activities. Check them out at www.davidfentonpublishing.co.uk

Dos and Don'ts of Google advertising.

Google represents the strongest form of advertising on the internet and must surely be worth taking advantage of. However there are areas where you can minimise your costs.

By getting involved as a Google sponsored advertiser, you bid for each click that somebody makes to get to your website.

Your clicks relate to keywords and it is important that the keywords chosen relate to your site.

The Google website is very sophisticated and you can start advertising your website very quickly with them.

www.google.com/adwords represents advertising that costs you money www.google.com/adsense represents google advertising on your site for you to **earn** money.

Check out the opportunities on both fronts.

If you have a niche market that has little competition but actually can provide compatible google advertising on your site then you could be making money just by people clicking on your site.

This is very much like a standard affiliate arrangement and can work very well with many different types of websites.

When using adwords, you have and advert that will attract visitors to your site.

Every time a prospect clicks on your site you pay Google an amount that you have agreed to opt for.

If you have submitted some very generic types of keywords that will bring thousands of hits to your site, you could be spending a fortune, onto find that you are not getting the conversions into sales.

For example, if you are selling left handed Golf Clubs and you use the keyword "Golf" you are going to get hundreds of visitors who, I have no doubt, are right handed Golfers with no interest in your product. The only way you will keep them there is to have a few affiliate links that you may earn some commission on.

Better to keep to long tailed keywords "Left handed Golf Clubs" bringing in fewer clicks but highly targeted worthy of conversion.

There is a google keyword planner tool that will tell you about how competitive a keyword is and also the number of times in an average month prospects click on that word. Google up "Google keyword planner tool"

Chapter 18 - How to produce your own video

Using videos in websites are very effective.

The process of such production is quite easy, once you have the tools to do it. Here are your basic requirements for a reasonably good quality website video.

A video camera that has..

1) A socket to take a U.S.B. cable

2) An HDMI socket

3) A video U.S.B. lead

4) Windows Movie Maker software or something compatible.

There are many varieties of Video Cameras about and you can spend a fortune shelling out for very sophisticated Video Cameras that will no doubt do the job. However, I have just purchased a perfectly good Panasonic second-hand one on E-Bay for £55 that is doing the job for me handsomely, so why pay £4-500 for the same effect?

Just check before purchasing that you have the above-mentioned sockets etc.

Taking the video shots

Don't get too hung up about getting it right first time.

Your camcorder should have a pause and go button

Use it to introduce the number of takes.

Press record and say "Take1" press Pause and get ready. Press Record

and then do the take. You may do number of takes before you get it right.

Your Movie maker software will enable you to do all sorts of editing and you may be able to combine takes to produce a very good video.

I found *Windows Movie Maker* really easy to use. Just a personal thing - you may find other software packages just as good.

Whatever you choose the editing process is much the same.

1) You need to connect your video mother board into your computer.

The thought of opening up a computer can be quite daunting. It felt quite scary for me but with the instruction details shown to me, I found the whole process of installation quite easy. Once the motherboard is in place and connected you will find that there will be a socket to take the firewire lead.

2) Connect the firewire lead to the camcorder and to the computer.

3) Switch the selection button on the camcorder to the section where you normally play/rewind etc.

4) Your computer should then acknowledge a connection.

5) Windows movie maker will then ask you to select the camcorder button.

6) A menu will then come up which shows you "capture video and "Finish"

7) You can then capture what you need on windows movie maker which will then produce for you a WMV file.

8) You can then go into Windows movie maker and import the file and edit according to the facilities available.

9) Once edited successfully you can then save the file/movie and give it a reference.

10) Now go into Webplus 8 or your Website production software

11) On your screen you will see tabs at the top showing "insert"

12) A sub menu will come down and you then need to click on to "Web" product

13) You will then get a menu showing you a browse button

14) Select the movie you require.

15) Select how you want your video to start - inline, etc.

16) Click the OK button and you will then have available a small logo square which your curser can place on whatever web page you have available with a single click.

You can then reduce to size.

17) Do a preview before uploading

18) Upload and check. Job done.

It takes a while to get used to playing around with the software so do not rush into things. Have fun with it.

Practice editing and seeing how versatile the system is.

You will find that it gets quite addictive so make sure you keep to your 2 or 3 hours at a time.

Chapter 19 - How to understand and produce a Blog

What is a Blog ?

Simply, a blog is really a Website that provides the opportunity for you to share information publicly about a particular subject.

Generally speaking interested visitors are invited to contribute their comments etc. to the Blog by way of accessing the site and typing in their comments.

Blogs can be very comprehensive and can attract many thousands of visitors

depending upon the subject matter. Here, therefore lies a wonderful opportunity to actually make some money by producing Blogs in such a way that will not only attract numerous visitors but will also signpost them to areas where they will make a purchase and you, in turn, either earn a commission

or make a sale.

There are certain "Blog" sites that can be produced free of charge.

Having now got our heads around understanding what a Blog is, let us now move on to producing a Blog that can earn you some money.

Blog production

Let's keep the costs down and go to www.blogger.com

Here you register for a free account. Just follow the easy instructions to create an account by clicking on the "create your Blog now" button.

On the following page you need to complete the form with your details.

You can then put in a Title that relates to your "niche" product. This is typed in to the Blog Title area and also into the Blog address area.

Once you have completed that section you can then click on to "settings".

Here you will be given a choice of templates to use.

Choose a template that you feel is suitable that sits nicely with your subject matter.

Each time click on the "continue" button.

You are now poised to put some interesting content into the Blog.

If you copied all the keywords from word tracker that relates to your subject matter, by including those words in your description or article you will attract more visitors because the "search engines" that Google use will seek out those words that now happen to be sitting on your Blog.

What you have done here is maximised the opportunity of getting visitors to come to your Blog because they have Googled up the relevant keyword.

Naturally, the Blog needs to be informative and enjoyable so that the visitor has a comfortable experience.

Let's recap at this stage.

You have pulled out the relevant keywords from Word Tracker

You have registered for a Blog account.

You have chosen a Template

You have written up a description or article that contains the keywords that You obtained from Word Tracker,

Now the visitor has a pleasant read. If the information is updated or changed on a regular basis, this makes for good reading and visitors are more likely to keep returning.

Here is our opportunity to start earning from having produced the Blog .

Now click on to the tab that says "customise" you will then have a template in front of you that provides you with a variety of choices.

Here if you click on "Add a Gadget" a menu will drop down showing you all the great things you can do to enhance your Blog.

One of these gadgets is "Link list"

Here is where, (after you have signed up to become an affiliate with the various companies you wish to represent), you put your given links to the websites that will guide your visitor to, hopefully, make a purchase which will earn you commission.

Once you have completed your Blog you need to ensure that the world is going to see what you have produced.

You now need to go to www.pingomatic.com

Just follow the simple instructions on this website that "pings" your Blog into the world wide web. Do this after every time you make any changes to your Blog, otherwise the visitors will only see the last "pinged" version.

If you Google up "How to produce a Blog" you will find other sources of Blog production. Keep looking around and don't be satisfied with just my own recommendation, although I have found www.blogger.com very easy to use.

If you keep looking for different subjects and products and get yourself affiliated to various companies, you could end up having hundreds of Blogs earning you money whilst you sleep.

You do need to persevere and keep repeating the process.

There are many people earning a very good living just by producing Blogs and updating them.

How to benefit from other websites

When you first start out with a product or service, look very carefully at other compatible websites.

For example, if you are selling Golf Clubs and another site is selling Golf Balls then it would be in your interest to contact that website owner for you both to swap html links.

Try to link with a website that is receiving lots of visits.

If you have a good niche product that is compatible with a larger popular website receiving thousands of hits, you could easily piggyback on the success of someone else.

Some websites provide advertising space at reasonable cost and it is up to you to negotiate further.

Small cost websites taking low cost advertising that can be targeted to various areas in the market sector are

Friday Ad, Facebook, Gumtree

I have no doubt there are others but I am only able to recommend those that I have used myself without fuss or bother.

Your "Other Website"

Sometimes it is prudent to run two websites offering the same product.

Different header and different title but same content.

Here you can monitor which is the better of the two receiving hits and then discard the weaker one.

Compatible affiliation also works well.

If you have your own website and you can put up an affiliate link to a compatible site that is not in competition with you, you have produced for yourself two bites of the cherry.

Your visitor browses your site. Not so keen but notices an attractive link and subsequently buys from where he/she was directed.

You then receive commission from that affiliate arrangement and your website helped to make it happen.

Chapter 20 - The Internet Selling Game

This session has been extracted from one of the many seminars that I have presented around the U.K. that has always been well received. If you are selling your products or services on the internet, the following pages of information will be of immense help to you.

Sales and selling is a subject matter in its own right and can take up the size of yet another book with many areas of advanced skills to learn.

However, for the purpose of getting you off to a flying start that enables you to "pick and mix" where your strengths and likes and dislikes are, I have kept it simple.

Each element is broken down as follows;

- Grab their attention
- Sell results- easy explanation of Features and Benefits
- The Motivating Key
- Call to action

You will find much of the following very useful if included in areas of your website.

Using A.I.D.A. combined with the above structure will help to increase conversions.

Attention - Grab their attention

Interest - Sell Results

Desire - The Motivating key

Action - Call to action

The whole sales process when broken down into these elements makes life much easier for you when you are producing your own sales copy.

You can purchase products/services with resell rights that often come with sales copy and all the marketing accessories. Here you really do not have to do anything other than put your own name to the product and sell it.

Don't stop improving the sales copy if you think its worthy of it.

If you are starting from scratch the following information will help you to produce good sales copy that generates business.

How to create good sales copy

Starting from the top. Your Title or header really must jump out at the reader and grab sufficient attention for them to read on.

If you are looking for prospects to buy a particular product such as a fishing rod, your title should be related with **results** and not about the features of the rod.

Bad example;

Get this carbon fibre rod at half price!

Good Example;

Catch double the fish at half the price with this super lightweight carbon fibre rod.

The first example is just selling another carbon fibre rod.

The second is going further by understanding **why** the reader wants to buy the rod in the first place.

There is, also, a greater sense of curiosity that comes from the second example coaxing the reader to find out more.

The first important rule of thumb, particularly when you wish to grab attention is to **sell results.**

We then slide into the "interest" section of the sales copy.

Having gained the reader's attention, you need to maintain it.

Here you can the start talking about the comparison of the new rod against others, the advantages it has. Beware of putting in features without benefits.

Example, Don't say "This rod has a much more flexible swing than other rods."

Say "This rod casts out much more easily because of its super flexible swing."

"The flexible swing" is what it has - (FEATURE)

"Casts out more easily" - is what it does (BENEFIT)

Start linking features and benefits together.

If you cannot think of a benefit that links to a feature then

don't bother mentioning it.

By this time your prospect should be warming up a little and the interest must not wane at this stage. More importantly it needs to increase to the point of the **big D** yes **Desire.**

Desire can only be brought about from what one reads by injecting some emotional **motivating key.** Something that motivates the reader to say "Wow, I want some of that".

What can we do to conjure up this motivating key?

Here are some examples;

Free Bait - worth £££

Free discount voucher - valued at £££

Free Membership - worth ££££

Notice **Free.** For the small amount of cost involved you can afford to throw something in that really converts the reader to make the purchase.

At this point the reader is wanting to buy and it is now up to you to make it easy for that to happen.

A **call to action** is needed and here are a few examples that will help you put that into place.

Buy now - limited time offer - ends (Date)

This price cannot be held for long - Full price returns in ten days.

It really is all about creating a sense of urgency.

When the reader has reached a desire stage, you are there to satisfy that desire (Session 1 - Marketing definition - Satisfaction/ Customer Requirements).

Online -

Press the "Buy now" button.

Complete this easy form for instant despatch

Pay now for instant download etc. etc.

Guarantee your product or service.

Buyers have their statutory rights but it is always beneficial to provide them with the peace of mind that they have a solid gold money back guarantee if dissatisfied.

Unfortunately, you will be met by a small percentage of "Takers" who will take advantage of your free offer and never buy anything from you or ask for their money back after gleaning the information.

Thankfully, most people are honest and they just want you to be honest also.

Chapter 21 - Using E-bay as an opportunity to sell

As Ebay represents a greater portion of my income and is a very effective selling platform for all kinds of services and products it is well worth studying the process of how I go about making such sales.

1) Get yourself a Paypal account. I did mention this in an earlier session.

Paypal is really a must when you get involved with Ebay.

Go to; www.paypal.com and sign up. It's free.

(2) You then need to sign up with Ebay at www.ebay.co.uk or www.ebay.com if you are outside of the U.K.

Go through the signing up procedure very carefully.

(3) Build up a credibility feedback before you really start selling.

The best way to start is to make some small low-priced purchases

of different items, then pay by paypal very promptly (You will need to put

some funds in)

You will then be given positive feedbacks from happy sellers.

Try to build up a 100% positive feedback of some 20 or 30 transactions before you go down the selling road.

Buyers look at sellers' feedbacks and that gives them confidence prior to making a purchase if they can see a top-quality seller with a 100% or near enough positive feedback.

You are now ready to sell- Do some research first.

Research

4) Pretend you are a buyer and type in the search window the item that you wish to sell.

5) click on to the advanced search button

6) tick the area that says "completed transactions"

You will then get a list of recent transaction that have taken place.

You will what was sold and what didn't sell

You will see what they were sold for. If you click on to one of the sold products, you will see how many people bid for the item.

This gives you a pretty good idea of what your product will fetch in the auction.

7) Click on to the "Sell" button

You will then be signposted to identify a particular category.

8) Click on your chosen category.

You will then be directed to a page where you proceed to complete bits of information about your product.

You will then be able to upload photographs of the product and complete a description of the product in the description box.

Good quality photographs are a must.

Obtain a good quality camera that has a socket for a U.S.B. lead.

It has a sign that looks like 3 wires.

I have a Camcorder that can take video filming and still photos.

If you are going to buy a Camcorder, get one that not only has the USB connection socket but also, very important, a DV socket that will allow you to upload videos to your computer as well.

Once you have good quality photos to upload to your Computer, ensure that you can get to them by labelling up a file called My Pictures or something.

(9) Follow the online instruction to upload your photo file under the "Enhanced" system of Ebay. Here you can then crop, rotate, improve contrast etc. before saving it to their site.

Once up, you have your first photo. Now on to the description.

(10) Here we go again - Use **A.I.D.A.**

Auction or Buy it Now

O.K. now to price.

I have found this area to be very interesting and I have found a great little tip that I will share with you to get people to bid.

Unless you go for a "Buy it Now" where they take it or leave it, I would recommend you put it to the auction section.

In the auction section there is also a "Buy it Now" opportunity.

For example, if you are selling a book and you would like to see something £20 into your Bank balance. You need to be clear about the value of the book to the customer in the description box. This may be £40 or £50.

I would suggest that you start at 4.99 with a "Buy it Now" price of £49.

You should not have paid more than a couple of pounds for the book in the first place but please be honest about the description.

Be thorough

Weight, size, age, colour, condition etc.

Your clients see a perceived value of around £50 and they are enticed to bid starting at a Fiver. You are in the running for getting around £20 to £30 based upon the above assumption.

Naturally it has to be comparable with your early research of completed transactions for the same type of item.

As soon as the bidding is over you can expect an immediate Paypal payment into your Paypal account.

As soon as that happens send a note of congratulations to your customer and advise them when you are going to despatch. Be quick and efficient.

You will get another positive feedback, this time from a Buyer.

If you are looking for physical products to resell on Ebay go for small high value items that are easy to post in padded Envelopes.

Items of Jewellery, Electronic items etc are a good start.

If you go into Ebay and type in Wholesale job lots. You will find a host of things to buy. You don't want to have a huge stock of stuff in your garage

That you cannot sell, so please check out all the options before you buy anything.

Go to Charity shops, Boot sales etc Table top sales, Jumble sales etc.

You will be amazed at what you can pick up and resell on Ebay.

If you are anything like me you will find it most addictive. I find it great fun.

After a while you should settle down to specialising in one or two areas that you find most satisfying and of course profitable.

Put all your energies into making those kinds of purchases and you will find that you will slowly make a name for yourself.

I specialise in Medical Exam books for Student Doctors, an extremely specialised niche area that has grown through one student recommending another.

You can do the same by identifying something a little specialised that people will look for.

To open your mind a little wider for what you can sell on Ebay, I happen to be a Karate Instructor in my local Town and I teach my students how to learn this Martial art from White Belt through to Black Belt. I took my Camcorder and my Wife filmed me going through every single session of learning.

The filming was then converted by me at home and then put on DVD (all done at home)

They were put into covers and printed up to look professional ending up with a DVD that sells at £3.95 post free in the UK

These are also being currently sold on Ebay with great success and I can afford to re-list them time and time again at such a low production cost of about 23p.

I am giving you this example because you may be good at something or knowledgeable about a particular subject and you can convey these ideas to people by selling them a set of DVDs or even a single DVD and start earning Money.

Did you know?

You can have an Ebay shop to handle up to 200 products costing you £30 month with FREE listing.

Let's recap. You can sell on Ebay

1) CDs that contain E-Book files for customers to download that you have re-packaged.

2) CDs as above containing your own production of E-Books offering Master Resell Rights to others.

3) Products that you have bought in wholesale and split up and put into smart boxes etc to increase the perceived value.

4) Information products - Hard copy form that you have produced from E-Books that you have downloaded.

5) Products that you have bought from Charity Shops, Car Boot Sales, Jumble sales, Table Top Sales.

6) CDs or DVDs from your own production from information and experience of your own.

You can make a living not unlike thousands of others just on Ebay alone.

Chapter 22 - Avoiding feast and famine times

Widening the net

My objective for you in this course is to ensure that you end up earning a reasonable living from home.

Being self employed, we hear, "has its ups and downs"

I call them "Peaks and "Troughs"

If the Troughs are still high enough for you to live on then it really doesn't matter much because you are making plenty during the peak periods.

However, invariably most people tend to virtually live off what they earn in peak periods and struggle during the troughs.

To try and even this out one must once again **anticipate.**

(Definition of Marketing - Chapter 1)

If you have an obvious seasonal product, please don't just go for gold in the peak time and hope that you will survive the troughs.

It never works! Let us just get on with something that does work.

Start launching a product that is designed to work during the trough period. Sounds very obvious doesn't it, but people just don't bother.

It may be that you take on an offline activity that brings you in positive cash flow that will tide you over during these periods. If not - start looking for it.

Be ahead of the game!

I got myself qualified as an Exercise to music Teacher and opened up another offline business that brings in a positive weekly cash flow.

I am very thankful for that because I don't have to worry about online troughs. (In fact, please see section 10 on joint ventures, because we are franchising that business out due to its success).

Another area of selection is to consider products or services that do not have seasonal trends, in which case you would be looking more at Food products, Health products, Animal Foodstuffs etc.

The opportunities are quite enormous and there are lots of producers out there looking for good marketers.

When we get into E-Book activities (session 9) you will learn more about looking for and selling the right sort of products.

You will note that I actually have a number of different income streams and I am constantly recycling them through "The Boston Matrix".

Providing you are doing the same you will not be a victim of a trough!

Understanding and using Niche Markets

A niche product is literally a product or service that fits neatly into a small corner of the market place happily making good profits with little competition.

When you check out Wordtracker and see a list that includes a product or service that has around 30/40 hits in a day, then it would be worth going into more research of that product by first going into Clickbank, key in the relevant name of the product or service and see what comes up.

If there is a supplier who is actively involved in selling the product and is also keen to employ you on an affiliate basis, then it is worthy of pursuing.

You may create your own niche market that relates to say a particular type of dog or cat, or any other animal. Assuming them to be pets, you can then extend that niche into foodstuffs, training and medical requirements. The potential opportunities are mind boggling.

Some niche products are so niche and so specialised you may not get much response. Here you would do well to either withdraw that product from your portfolio or go the other way and create a large number of small niche products. Don't forget you need to manage the updating of these products so if you find the volume sales are slow, you need to be sure that there is a high level of profit to be made.

To help you get to grips with selection of niche products, here is a guideline of how to go about it.

Let us look at the equestrian Market sector.

Start with say - Horse Riding

Go to www.www.wordtracker.com/freekeywords

You will then be shown the keyword window and "Hit me" button.

Key in **Horse Riding**

You will find 34 searches made - Nice little niche area.

Then go to

www.paydotcom.com

Go straight to "Market place"

Key in "Horse Riding"

Low and behold there is a guide being produced and ready to sell just on that subject together with giveaway bonuses etc..

Retails at $37 with a 60% commission = $22.20 that's around £14.

All you need to do is promote that in the form of a website or Blog and include it in with other niche products for horses etc. and ensure that visitors come to your site, knowing that they will have a specific requirement.

A Great winter way of earning money from buyers who want to know how to ride a horse "**In the comfort of their own home** "

Another ready-made little business for you.

Link selling and cross promotions

You can extend your niche product sales by Link selling and cross promotions.

Take the above-mentioned Horse Riding Lessons for example.

Google up **Horse Riding**

Up will come a host of websites and information.

You can then select compatible websites that will be worth contacting to share a link with your website or you can advertise your guide on their website etc. Here you have **cross promoted.**

Link selling is where you have already sold a product to one of your clients and you have subsequently offered another product or service that **links up** with their original purchase.

e.g.

You have sold them a guide on "how to train yourself to do Horse Riding".

Two weeks later you come up with an offer for some equestrian products

that are vital for safe and efficient Horse Riding.

Cross Promotions are great to further expand the exposure of your business.

Link selling is great to ensure retention of customer interest.

Chapter 23 - Running your own profitable seminars

An excellent offline way of promoting your business is to attract delegates who are willing to pay to come to a venue and learn directly from you.

If you really know your subject well, to the extent that you can write articles and/or E-Books etc. about it, you could supplement that income by setting up a series of seminars during the course of 12 months.

One important factor when it comes to seminar work is that the delegates need to be able to take something home with them that has made their day worthwhile.

Sometimes one or two ideas alone is all that is needed. You will, of course, will be presenting a number of different ideas to your audience and they then have the opportunity of using all or some of them.

Another area of importance is the way you present yourself to a group of people. There are many clients of mine who really do know their subject well but do not possess the quality of injecting enthusiasm into others or have the confidence to address 20 /30 people at once.

Presentation and confidence skills are of paramount importance here.

Let us assume that you possess such qualities.

We need to plan. Here is the guide;

1) If you have your subject matter in place, contact a variety of Hotels in the target area.

2) Ask for quotations for a meeting room to cater for 50 people, 20

   people, 10 people.

   Good Hotels have a range of different rooms to cater for different

   numbers of people.

3) Ask to be quoted for Morning and afternoon Coffees and Fixed price Lunch.

4) Find out when the nearest cancellation without penalty date is.

Generally Hotels may take details of your credit card at that stage without actually billing you, as a means of confirmation of booking.

If you are running a seminar such as "Customer Care" invite their staff via the Hotel Manager to a discount opportunity.

With all those parameters in place set to work with your costings to include a break even point.

Here is an example:-

Cost of room for 50 delegates:-	£150.00
Cost per delegate Lunch & Coffees	£ 18.00
Cost of materials for each delegate	£ 5.00
Assuming 25 delegates turn up total cost =	£725.00
Charge out rate for each delegate	= £77.00
25 delegates @ £77 each =	£1925.00
Gross profit for the day =	**£1200.00**

Let's go smaller shall we:-

Cost of Room Hire for 10 delegates	=	£80.00
Cost per delegate lunch & Coffees	=	£18.00
Cost of materials for each delegate	=	£ 5.00

Assuming 8 delegates turn up total cost £264.00

Charge out rate for each delegate = £ 77.00

8 delegates @ £77 each = £616.00

Gross profit for the day = £352.00

Your break even point for the small room is approx. 1.5 delegates.

You will need to consider what you feel is the minimum number of delegates that you will need to make it worth your while.

Consider

1) Your preparation time

2) Preparation of Materials

3) Your travelling time and costs

4) Possible overnight accommodation

Some dos and don'ts on presentation:

Please try and make your seminars as interactive as possible.

Split the delegates into working groups etc.

Don't overdo the powerpoint presentation. A flipchart is very useful.

Don't use too many slides.

Clearly outline your objectives from the off.

Put up on the flipchart your delegates objectives for the day.

Target yourself to meet those objectives.

Maintain your enthusiasm throughout the day.

Do not get involved with lengthy discussion with one delegate.

Disagree in a constructive way without embarrassment.

Encourage and motivate audience participation.

The more they do the more they like it.

Ensure you get feedback forms completed.

If agreeable by all, get the seminar videoed.

Get agreement for the video to be used to promote other seminars.

Offer discounts and bonuses in voucher form for further recommendations.

Use the seminar as a "Sprat to catch a Mackerel"

Seminars are wonderful environments to really build up a relationship with your clients.

If you are observant enough you will be able to identify those delegates who have a yearn to improve or gain more knowledge etc. and clearly the one day seminar is just not nearly enough for them.

They have a need, somewhat dormant at present, perhaps.

You task is to wake it up.

Here is your chance to move in and offer on a more personal basis- personal tuition or advanced tuition or something of greater depth with your help etc.

This is then costed by the hour and you are then able to look at a much higher income.

Such Sprats are also used often online.

Free bonuses. Free gifts. All these are Sprats.

See every client as a potential Mackerel.

Chapter 24 - Understanding E-Books

What is an E-Book?

Let's get that out of the way first shall we?

An E-Book is an electronic version of a hard copy book.

It is in a computer file and as such can be downloaded, read and printed off.

You can purchase E-Books via www.Ebay.co.uk who, up till recently had a variety of sellers who would sell you a range of these books that you could instantly download. Ebay rules have changed somewhat but you can still buy E-books that are sent to you on a C.D. and you can upload the files that way.

If you go to www.clickbank.com you can buy and sell E-books and be an affiliate. Everything is digital on click bank.

Cost of E-Books are very reasonable. Look out for those that offer you genuine "Reseller rights."

Reseller Rights

Such rights provide you with the opportunity to repackage the whole thing under your own name as a Publisher and resell for 100% of the profits.

Look for "niche" subjects. These are more specialised areas that fetch higher prices.

Be creative! You can even bring different E-Books together to form your own book and repackage it.

Spend a small amount of money on a binding machine.

Print off your newly edited version and put it together as a proper hard copy book.

The fact that you are putting yourself out and making the effort saves other people an awful lot of time and they are quite prepared to pay the price for something that is relevant to their interest.

Your efforts, however are only going to be for the very first book. Save all the details and all you have to do from then on is to copy everything. Low cost, high profits to be made.

You can even buy large job lots of E-Books at very low prices including a host of articles on loads of different subjects.

I have many hundreds of these that I have bought over the last 3 years and I always have a stock of opportunities at my disposal.

If you Google up "(Golf) resell rights"

You will get a complete listing of E-Book on Golf that you can purchase.

Just replace "Golf" with your chosen subject to get E-Books that you are looking for.

Having covered the "Resell Rights" handling and selling other peoples E-Books and repackaging etc., you can also produce your own E-Book

If you have an interest that you have been involved with for some time, you would do well to document it and put it into some kind of publishing framework. You would be surprised as to how many people will be happy to buy information based upon your own experience.

You could then offer others "Resell Rights". In your E-Book you could make a reference to any websites you may have that relate to the subject matter where a purchase could be made.

You could put various links in the E-Book to any of your relevant affiliate links.

The reason behind this is that if you offer "Resell rights" to your clients who buy the E-Book from you. They in turn can resell to others. That opens up a wide area of people reading your book that increases the opportunities of more visitors to your website or affiliate website, thus providing you with a residual income for no real effort.

When constructing your EBook you need to use the A.I.D.A. method and ensure that the body of your book is interesting and informative.

If you are selling a physical product you could offer a free E-Book.

Left handed Golf Clubs with a Free E-Book on Golf Tips etc.

A Fishing Rod with a Free E-Book on best Bait for Catching Fish.

The opportunities here are only limited to the extent of your own imagination.

If that dries up, go to a Newsagent and take a look at all the specialist Magazines and take a note of all the Titles. A wide range of subjects that people buy off the shelf.

But there are many more Magazines that are available by subscription only.

To give you an idea of the full range of Magazines available go to

www.mediauk.co.uk

Here you will find hundreds of magazines covering oodles of subjects. Not only does this give you inspiration for ideas to work on but also you can advertise in these Magazines at reasonable cost and they are generally thoroughly read by specific targeted audiences.

Creating your own E-Book will provide you with a great deal of personal satisfaction once achieved but it is much quicker to earn money by just re-packaging a "Resell Rights" E-Book and sell on.

There are also numerous "copyright free" publications that you could alter slightly or re-package and re-market them.

Chapter 25 – Accounts made easy

If you wish to become a Ltd company your liability is restricted to the activities of the company and your annual accounts are available to the general public. The services of an accountant are recommended in this instance.

If you are trading as either a sole proprietor or a partnership in a non Ltd environment then both you and your partner are personally liable for the financial activities of the business.

Our business is a husband and wife partnership and we are VAT registered but not a Ltd company.

I have carried out all the accounts myself, including VAT returns and found this very easy to do using Express Accounts from …

www.nchsoftware.com/accounting/index.html

There are numerous accounts packages available but I have found NCH very good value for money.

Whatever package you choose. Do start early as you will need to enter a number of items of expenditure during your setting up process.

I enter sales and purchases where applicable everyday. My philosophy is "Do it now" and the "In Tray" is never over-loaded.

There is much here for you to get your teeth into and make a great start.

The **Essentials** that have been covered are

Sales, Marketing, Advertising, Presentation skills, Internet, Accounts

Please feel free to contact me re any questions you have that are relevant to the content of this book. Email is by far the best as I do

have a very busy life and you can be assured of an answer by using this method.

You can contact me through dave@davidfentonpublishing.co.uk

My best wishes for your future success

David Fenton

Why not join

David Fenton Associates

To keep your business up to date and ahead of the competition.

Find out more at

www.davidfentonassociates.co.uk